TIME TRAVEL SLEEPOVER

KNIGHTS & CASTLES

EAT, SLEEP AND PARTY
IN THE MIDDLE AGES!

WRITTEN BY
TIMOTHY KNAPMAN

ILLUSTRATED BY
MATT ROBERTSON

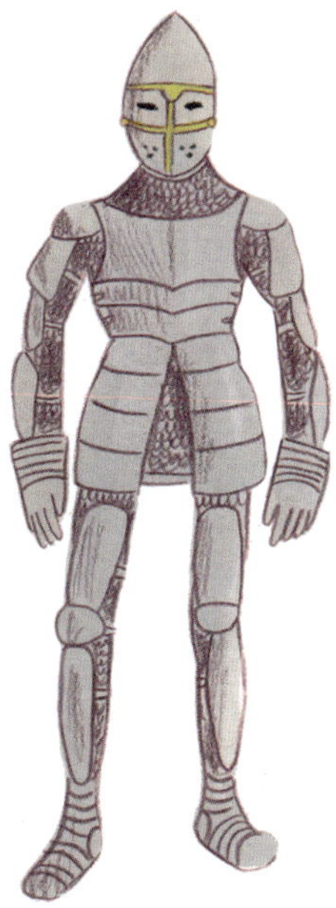

happy yak

To Christopher and Charlotte with love – T. K.

To Will and Kitty – M. R.

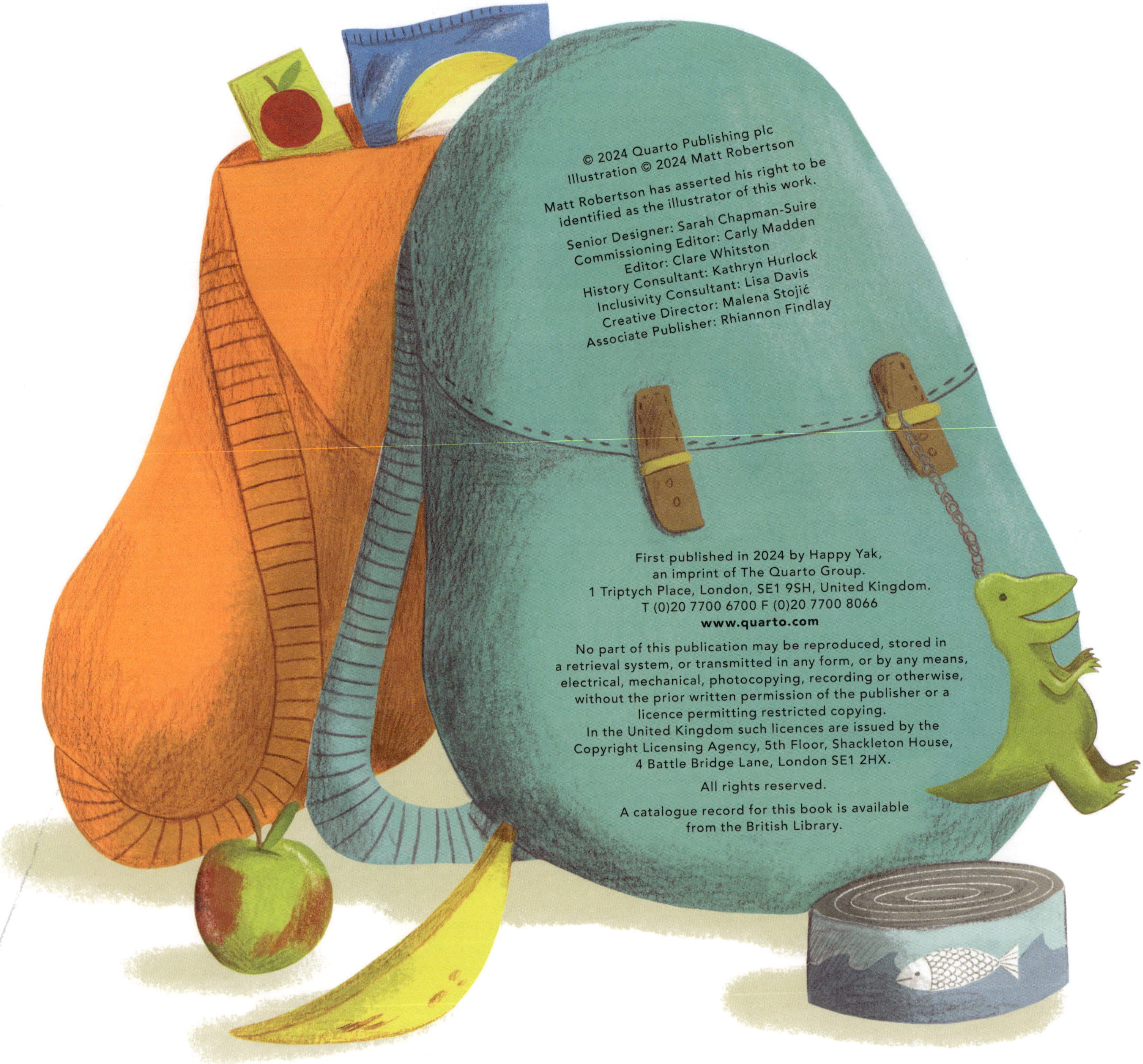

Matt Robertson has asserted his right to be identified as the illustrator of this work.

Senior Designer: Sarah Chapman-Suire
Commissioning Editor: Carly Madden
Editor: Clare Whitston
History Consultant: Kathryn Hurlock
Inclusivity Consultant: Lisa Davis
Creative Director: Malena Stojić
Associate Publisher: Rhiannon Findlay

First published in 2024 by Happy Yak,
an imprint of The Quarto Group.
1 Triptych Place, London, SE1 9SH, United Kingdom.
T (0)20 7700 6700 F (0)20 7700 8066
www.quarto.com

A catalogue record for this book is available from the British Library.

MIX
Paper | Supporting responsible forestry
FSC® C016973

ISBN 978 0 7112 8726 6

Manufactured in Guangdong, China TT042024
9 8 7 6 5 4 3 2 1

CONTENTS

Say hello to our TIME-TRAVELLERS!

JAKE

Interests: stomping around in armour, making a lot of noise

If you could go anywhere in history: I'd go to the Middle Ages, and be a knight

What you hope to get from this adventure: I'd like to give jousting a try!

LULA

Interests: having an adventure, of course!

If you could go anywhere in history: I'd go to a time where kids got to charge around on horseback

What you hope to get from this adventure: to find out what knights were REALLY like!

CLAWDIA

Interests: lying on sunny windowsills

If you could go anywhere in history: I'd go somewhere with a lot of mice

What you hope to get from this adventure: a bellyful of mice

Are you ready?
Time travel's easy – you just have to do THE TIME-TRAVEL SHIMMY.
You do a little wiggle and...
...you touch the ground.
Then wrinkle your nose while you spin around.

HERE WE GO!:
KNIGHTS AND CASTLES

Our friends have travelled back to the Middle Ages – the time of knights and castles!

“They don’t seem to like cats much around here,” says Jake.

“Maybe they’re allergic,” says Lula.

“Cats are thought to bring bad luck,” explains one child.

“But they’re also useful for catching mice,” says another. “Anyway, *we* like cats.”

“Welcome to the Middle Ages!”

“Our cat’s called Clawdia,” says Lula. “I’m Lula and this is Jake.”

“I’m Eloise and this is my brother Hubert,” says the girl.

“The Baron, who owns this castle, has just returned home,” says Hubert. “There’s going to be a feast tonight to celebrate. Everyone is very busy!”

STUFF WE'LL NEED

- BACKPACKS
- JUICE CARTONS
- PLASTERS

(KNIGHTS HAVE SWORDS AND THEY CAN BE SHARP!)

- EMERGENCY CAT FOOD

(CLAWDIA GETS MOODY WHEN SHE HASN'T EATEN)

Whoosh!

You shake your hips.

Then you jump off the ground.

And just like that...

MEET THE FAMILY

LIFE IN THE CASTLE

Lula and Jake meet Eloise and Hubert's parents. Their mother is called Juliette and their father is François – the Baron's steward.

"Can't talk!" says François. "Too busy! It's my job to run the castle for the Baron and make sure he gets everything he wants!"

"I suppose you mean things like really big swords, shining armour and fancy horses?" asks Jake, eagerly.

"No – it's something way more difficult than that. He wants... a bath... with hot water!" says Juliette.

There is a **mews** for the Baron's falcons, and **stables** for his horses.

You've got a wishing well!
It's also useful for when the Baron wants a bath. Most people have to go for a dip in the river.
This well means we'll always have a water supply, even if the castle is under siege.
Keep
Herbs are grown in the walled garden to use in cooking and medicine.
Fruit trees and the fishpond supply food.
Inner Bailey
Can't catch me!
It's breakfast time, mouse. I'm saving you for lunch!
Moat

MAKE YOURSELF AT HOME

INSIDE THE CASTLE

Eloise and Hubert invite Lula and Jake inside the castle keep. The keep is the centre of the castle and the safest place to be.

"It's very cold and dark," says Jake. "Where's the light switch?"

"They don't have electricity," says Lula. "Or central heating – brrr!"

"We use candles for light, fire for heat and wall hangings to keep the draughts out," says Hubert.

"No wonder it's so hard to keep warm!" says Jake.

GOOD NEWS!

Castles had toilets, called garderobes.

BAD NEWS!

They were just holes in the floor, covered with planks of wood.

GOOD NEWS!

They were high up so anything smelly fell a long way down.

BAD NEWS!

Watch out if you're underneath it when it lands!

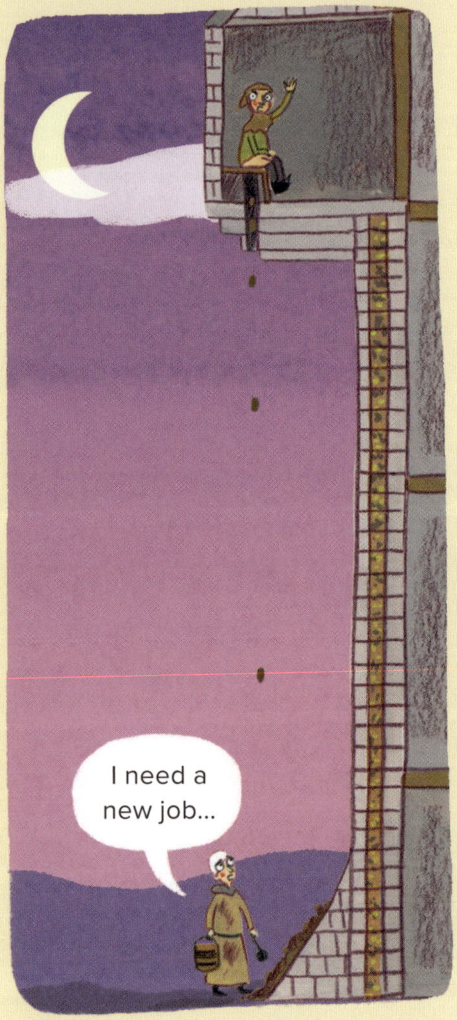

When there was enough waste, the poo was taken away at night by someone called a gong farmer, who then sold it to farmers to fertilize their fields.

Not too hot, remember! We want to wash the Baron, not cook him.
Let's hope he doesn't want another bath soon – that's the last of the roses!
The water takes so long to heat that some people even have baths together!
Share my bubble bath? No thanks!
Baron's Bedchamber
This winding staircase is making me dizzy! Where are we going again?
Up!
Chapel
Great Hall
Spiral Staircase
Storeroom
I am Tibert, the castle cat. Want some help with that mouse?
I was doing very well on my own, thank you.

MAKEOVER TIME!

CLOTHES AND HAIRSTYLES

While the Baron is in the bath, the kids sneak into his chambers to look at his clothes.

"You'll need clothes from our time if you want to blend in," says Eloise.

"What does everyone else wear?" asks Jake.

"They have a simpler outfit they wear every day," says Hubert.

"It's a hoodie – cool! But what's it made of?" asks Jake.

"Rough wool and linen, so it's very itchy," says Hubert.

GOOD NEWS!

You're a well-dressed young man in the Middle Ages!

BAD NEWS!

Your super-cool pointy shoes – called crakows – are impossible to walk in.

GOOD NEWS!

Your super-short tunic is very fashionable.

BAD NEWS!

Your tunic is so short, your bum gets cold!

KNIGHTS' CLOBBER

DRESSED TO KILL

Jake and Lula can't wait any longer to find out about suits of armour, so Hubert and Eloise take them to try some on.

1. First you wear a gambeson – a quilted shirt filled with feathers.

2. Over that, a shirt of chain mail. You roll it on, like a woolly jumper.

3. Then the coat of steel plates.

4. Then the helmet.

5. Finally, the surcoat to keep the sun off your armour.

Each piece of armour has a special name.

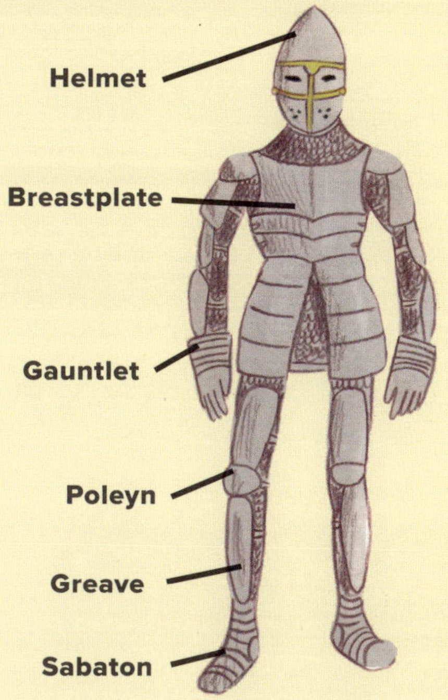

Knights wear special armour for jousting (fighting on horseback for sport and honour).

The shoulder plate protects a knight from their opponent's lance.

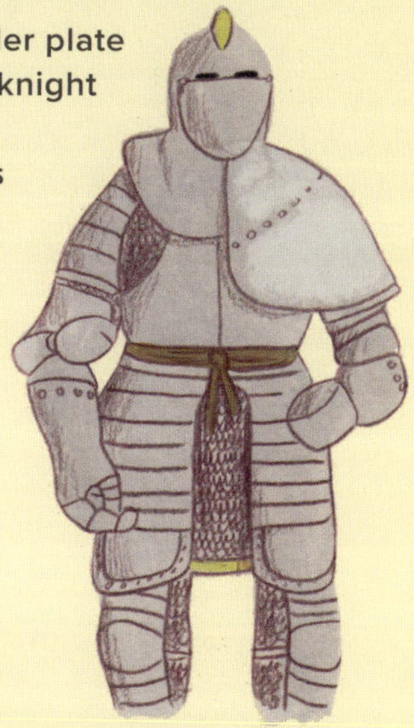

"Some armour allowed a knight to be screwed into their saddle so they wouldn't fall off," Hubert says.

"But that's cheating!" Lula says.

"That's what the King thought, so he banned it."

IN THE OLDEN DAYS

CASTLES OLD AND NEW

Like armour, castles are built for protection.

"This castle's been here for hundreds of years," says Eloise.

"But it hasn't always looked like this," says Hubert.

Pierre, a groom in the castle stables, overhears them. "You can say that again!" he chuckles. "My family's been working in this castle from the beginning. When we first came here, this castle was just a heap of earth. Literally... "

Can't blow it down now! They rebuilt the castle out of stone. Now the castle is bigger, and much more secure.
They're using that wheel to bring up the heavy stones.
Those poor people have to keep it going round, like hamsters!
After wearing all that heavy armour, I don't even want to think about carrying those big stone blocks!

UNDER ATTACK!

DEFENDING THE CASTLE

Jake and Lula ask what would happen if the castle was attacked. François is still busy ordering people about, but he is an expert on defending the castle so he stops to explain.

"The attackers use catapults to throw heavy objects to break down the castle. This trebuchet can chuck large blocks over 300 metres!" says François.

"So what do you do?" asks Lula.

"Duck!" shouts François.

"Sometimes attackers try to smash the front door down with a battering ram, but defenders can throw boiling oil from the gatehouse," says François.

"I think I'd decide to call again another day," says Jake.

"How do knights defend the castle?" Jake asks.

"They fight on horseback, and that's not much use in a siege," says Hubert.

"But castles have a secret back door," says François, "so that soldiers, including knights, can sneak out and ambush the attackers from behind."

"Ripples on the water in this bowl tell us that someone's tunnelling under the castle to plant a bomb," explains François.

"I just thought the defenders might need a wash," says Jake.

"A belfry, or siege tower, can hold hundreds of soldiers, protecting them until they pour over the battlements," says François.

"Archers firing flaming arrows might be able to deter the enemy before they reach the castle walls," says Eloise.

WE'RE HUNGRY!

EXPLORING THE KITCHEN

Jake and Lula have been very busy this morning. Now, their tummies are rumbling.

"The castle kitchens will be very busy," says Eloise. "They're preparing for tonight's feast to celebrate the Baron's return."

There is no breakfast. People ate a meal between 10 am and 11 am in the morning and another one between 4 pm and 5 pm in the afternoon.

There are no fridges or freezers. Fish and meat are preserved by covering them in salt. Milk lasts longer if it's turned into cheese.

The Baron and his family eat pandemain – white bread, made from wheat flour that has been sifted two or three times. Most people eat darker bread made with rye flour.

Large animals are roasted over open fires. They have to be turned constantly – it's hard work!

Most people eat pottage (thick vegetable soup), bread, milk, cheese and a little bacon.

GOOD NEWS!

It's dinner time in the Middle Ages!

BAD NEWS!

There are no forks and no plates – people use knives and spoons and eat off pieces of stale bread called trenchers.

GOOD NEWS!

There's less washing up!

KNIGHT SCHOOL

PART ONE: PAGE TO SQUIRE

It's too hot in the kitchen for Lula and Jake. They go outside to cool off and see two knights practising sword fighting.

"I want to become a knight," says Jake.

"And me!" says Lula. "I bet I'd make a better knight than you!"

"Becoming a knight takes time," says Hubert, "and you start young..."

Age 7–13 You are sent to a rich household to be a page. Pages have to run errands and learn to obey orders...

Age 14–21

If you keep your temper for all those years as a page, you get to be a squire. A squire is a knight's personal assistant and looks after their armour, weapons...

KNIGHT SCHOOL

PART TWO: LEARNING SKILLS

Jake and Lula are fed up with having to look after their knights all the time.

"When do WE get to do the fun stuff?" asks Jake.

"Being a squire isn't just about taking care of your knight," says Hubert. "You are also training to become a knight yourself one day."

"But it's hard work," says Eloise. "You need to be fit and strong."

The Ceremony

At last, when squires are about 21 years old and have mastered all the skills required, they are made knights in a special ceremony.

The night before, the squire has a nice, cold bath.

Then the squire puts on a white tunic and stays up all night praying in the castle chapel.

The next morning, the squire kneels before their lord, who 'dubs' them by touching their shoulder or neck with the blunt side of a sword.

TIME FOR SCHOOL!

LESSONS

Becoming a knight turns out to be much harder than Jake and Lula expected.

"Maybe going to school would be easier than training to be a knight," says Jake. "As long as we don't have to do hard sums."

"You'd prefer lessons to quintain practice?" says Hubert.

"You don't get bashed on the head with a heavy sandbag at school," says Lula.

"Maybe not," says Eloise, "but the castle chaplain who teaches us is very strict."

The children of craftspeople, such as carpenters or stonemasons, learn their trades by helping their families.

Like the children of merchants, the children of craftspeople also learn enough reading, writing and arithmetic (sums) so they can keep business records.

GOOD NEWS!

You're a successful stonemason. People want you to decorate important buildings.

BAD NEWS!

You need to work out how much money to charge for the work, but you don't have a calculator.

GOOD NEWS!

You can use a wooden counting frame called an abacus instead.

BAD NEWS!

It can only do simple calculations – it can't help with hard sums!

Schooling outside the home is often run by the Church. A lot of teaching is done by priests, and occasionally monks and nuns.

"What's this language?" says Jake.

"It's Latin, which is the language we're taught in and the language of the Catholic Church. It's understood in many countries," says Eloise.

"In class, we might still talk in our own language, but the teachers don't like it," says Hubert.

The children of privileged people such as kings, queens and barons are taught at home by personal tutors. Less attention is paid to the education of girls, though they are still taught how to run a household and care for people.

Sometimes, girls are taught in nunneries. Girls who become nuns have the option to continue their studies for the rest of their lives and some go on to make great contributions to knowledge.

OUT IN THE FIELDS

WORKING THE LAND

Most children don't go to school at all. Instead, they work outside all day, looking after the crops. Now the crops are ripe, everyone is busy harvesting them.

"It looks like such hard work!" says Jake.

"You think putting your socks on is hard work," says Lula.

The land beyond the castle walls is split into three large fields. Each field is divided into thin strips.

One field is left 'fallow', with no crops growing in it, to allow the land to rest.

People can rent strips of land in each field from the Baron in order to grow their own food.

There are woods too, for people to gather firewood to heat their homes.

A tithe (or a tenth of all the food) must be given to the local church to support the priest. Some priests have their own farms, but they still get tithes. This food is stored in a special tithe barn.

"So as well as paying the Baron to grow their food, and working on his land, they also give a tenth of everything to the Church?" says Jake.

"Yes, and if you steal an animal to eat from the Baron's land, it's called poaching. That is a very serious crime," says Eloise.

Farm workers aren't allowed to leave the area they live and work in – it's against the law!

There is also common land where animals can graze.

Once the crops are harvested, they are tied up and stored in barns to preserve them.

OUCH!

GOING TO THE DOCTOR

Lula has hurt her finger and needs a plaster – but they don't have plasters in the Middle Ages!

"We have treatments for all sorts of diseases," says Hubert.

"Do they work?" asks Lula.

"Erm... sometimes," says Eloise.

"We are lucky because we can see the baron's personal doctor, called a physician," says Hubert.

"We believe that four bodily fluids, called humours, control what sort of person you are – cheerful, grumpy, sad or quiet. People get ill when their humours are out of balance," says the physician.

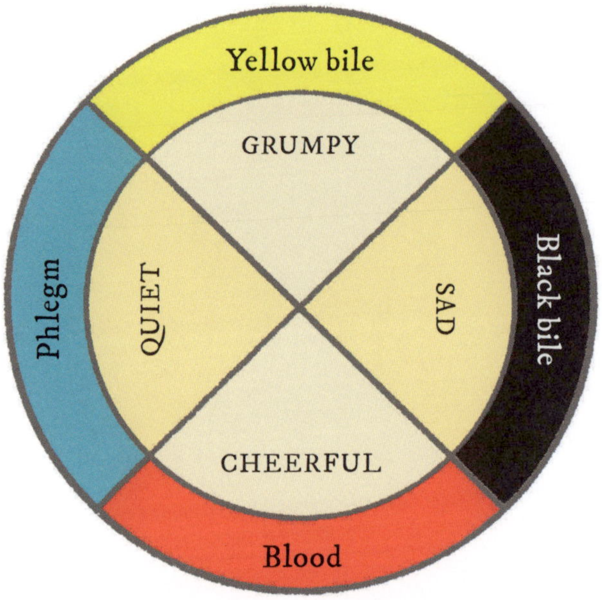

Doctors thought they could tell which humour a patient had too much of by looking at their wee.

BAD NEWS!

You're ill in the Middle Ages.

GOOD NEWS!

The doctor doesn't think you have a problem with your humours. Instead, they blame your illness on 'miasma' or BAD AIR.

BAD NEWS!

To get rid of bad air, you need even worse air, so they make you sit on a dung heap.

Want an operation? Go to the hairdresser!

In the Middle Ages, hairdressers did more than cut hair – they did operations, too! Today, a few barbers' shops still have a red and white pole outside. The red represents blood and the white represents bandages!

PICK A JOB!

FIGHT OR WORK?

Being a squire was a lot less fun than Jake and Lula had hoped, and they didn't enjoy working in the fields either. They know all about craftspeople, nuns and doctors now, so what other jobs are there in the Middle Ages?

"Maybe I could run a leech farm?" says Jake.

"You can't just choose any job you like. There are many rules that we all follow," says Eloise. "Most people must do the same job as their parents."

"That's not fair!" says Jake.

"This is the Middle Ages, remember – nothing is fair," says Lula.

"Jobs are divided into three groups..." says Hubert.

Those Who Fight

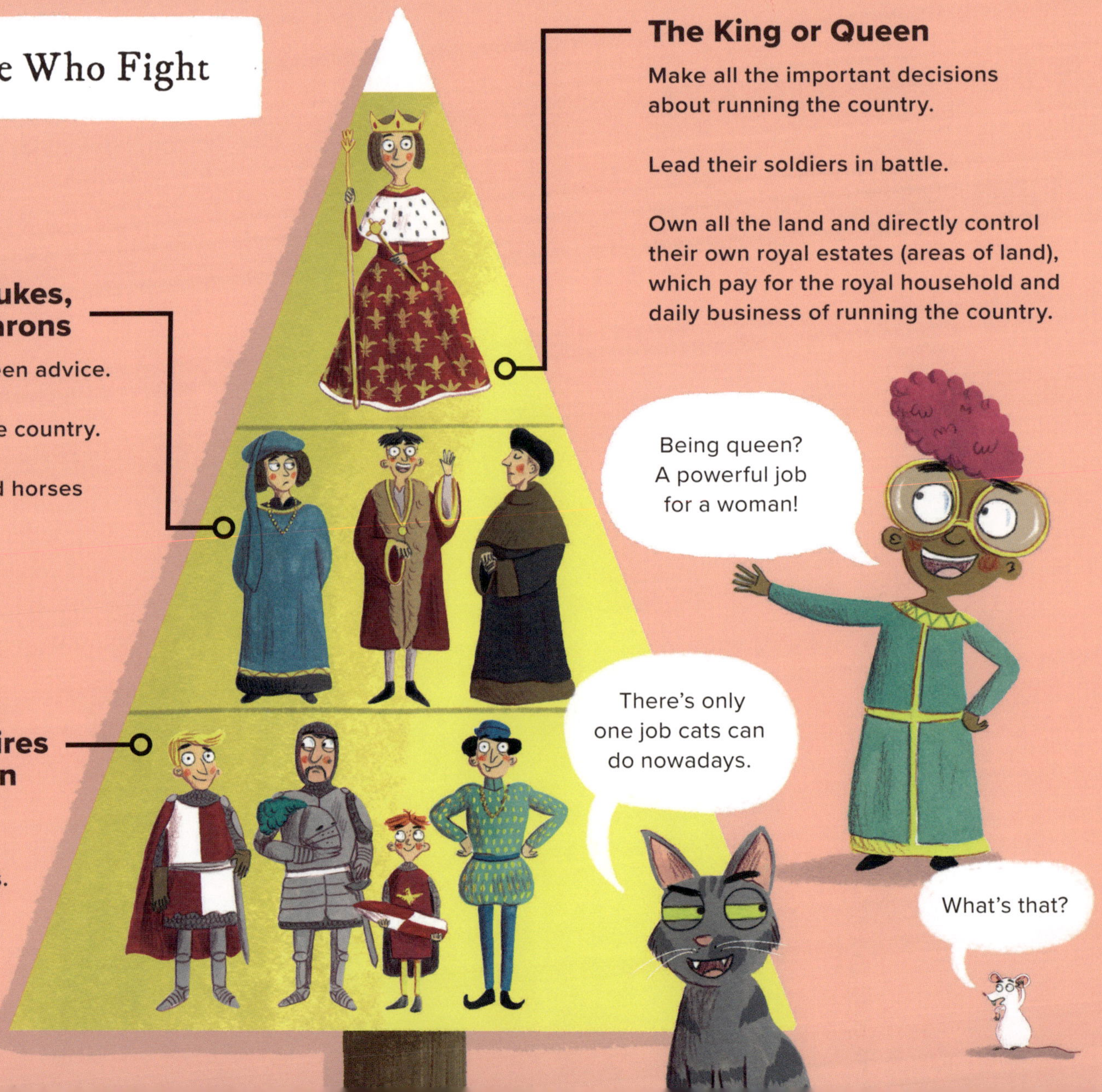

The King or Queen

Make all the important decisions about running the country.

Lead their soldiers in battle.

Own all the land and directly control their own royal estates (areas of land), which pay for the royal household and daily business of running the country.

The Peers – Dukes, Counts and Barons

Give the king or queen advice.

Help run parts of the country.

Provide soldiers and horses in time of war.

Knights, Esquires and Gentlemen

Trained soldiers or lords of manors with smaller estates. They pay taxes to the royal family.

Those Who Work

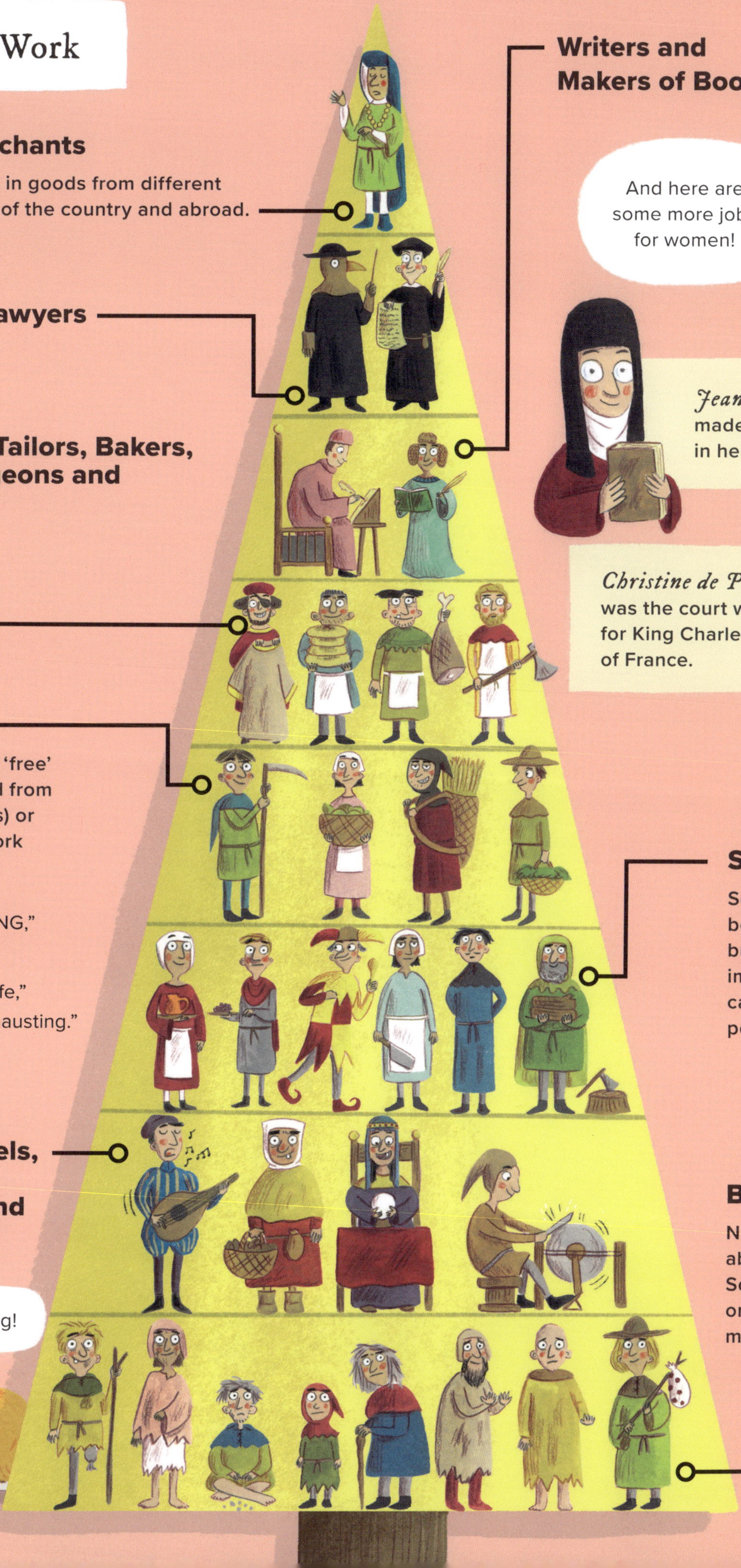

Merchants

Trade in goods from different parts of the country and abroad.

Physicians and Lawyers

Shopkeepers, Tailors, Bakers, Butchers, Surgeons and Craftspeople

Farm Workers

Farm workers are either 'free' (they rent their own land from the Baron and pay tithes) or 'unfree' (they have to work the Baron's land).

"I did that. It's EXHAUSTING," says Jake.

"Try doing it your whole life," says Hubert. "THAT'S exhausting."

Travelling Minstrels, Salespeople, Fortune-tellers and Knife-sharpeners

Writers and Makers of Books

Jeanne de Montbaston made beautiful books in her workshop in Paris.

Christine de Pizan was the court writer for King Charles VI of France.

Servants

Servants might get bossed around, but the servants of important people can boss other people around too!

Beggars

Not everyone was able to get a job. Some had to depend on asking people for money and food.

WORKING FOR GOD

THOSE WHO PRAY

Jake and Lula have noticed how many religious buildings there are in the Middle Ages and they want to know more.

People follow many different religions all over the world, including Islam and Judaism. In this part of Europe, most people are Christians and worship in churches. They ask the Baron's chaplain – his personal priest – to explain more.

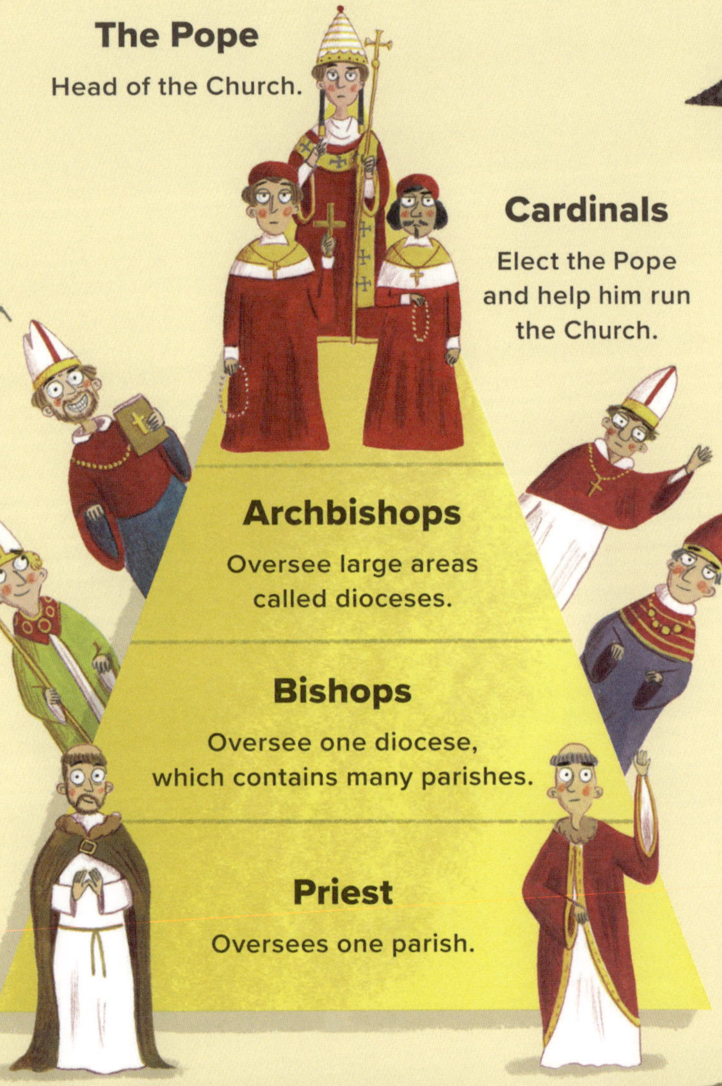

Cathedrals

Abbeys, Monasteries and Nunneries

Some men become monks and some women become nuns. They live in religious communities. They study, worship and help to take care of those in need.

Parish Church

Every village has its own church where people gather regularly for worship. It is where church-goers are baptised, married and buried.

The walls and windows of a church are decorated with statues and pictures – telling stories from the Bible for people who can't read.

The German nun, Hildegard of Bingen, wrote poetry and music, and made discoveries in science and medicine.

GOOD NEWS!

You've decided to become a monk. You can study and serve the community.

BAD NEWS!

That means you've promised to live a simple life with no luxuries.

GOOD NEWS!

Although you don't have money, your monastery does. Over time, people have given it so much money and land that you'll still live very well!

TOP OF THE HEROES

LEGENDARY KNIGHTS

Sir Eustace, the Baron's bravest knight, comes riding by on his horse.

"He looks so cool," says Jake.
"Maybe I'd still like to be a knight after all."

Eloise introduces Lula and Jake to Sir Eustace.

"Why did you become a knight?" Lula asks.

"Because of all the wonderful stories of knights I was told when I was your age," he answers. "Here are my favourites. See which you like best."

KING ARTHUR

In his castle, Camelot, there was a Round Table for his knights to sit at. The table was round to show that all the knights were equal.

SIR LANCELOT

Bravest of the Knights of the Round Table, and King Arthur's best friend, until love drove him to break his oath of loyalty to King Arthur.

SIR GALAHAD

The purest of the knights, he succeeded in the greatest quest and found the Holy Grail.

ST GEORGE
HELP!
Rescued a princess from a fearsome dragon.
SIEGFRIED
Bathed in dragon's blood, which protected him from attack, but a leaf fell on his back and that patch became his weak spot.
I am a dragon! ROARRR!!
Well, we're not knights! Run!
Look! Girls are just as brave as boys.
There are stories of brave warriors, just like knights, from all over the world.
MUIRISC
Legendary ruler in Ireland. Renowned for her courage, she was a famous warrior, sea captain and leader of men.
HUA MULAN
When war came to China, her father was too old to fight, so she took his place. Hua Mulan fought bravely for 10 years. The Emperor wanted to reward her but she just wanted to go home.
THE AMAZONS
Fearsome female warriors in Greek mythology. Skilled in archery, horse riding and war, they lived at the edge of the known world.

KNIGHTS AROUND THE WORLD

HEROES EVERYWHERE

As Lula and Jake have seen, tales of brave warriors are told all over the world.

"Wow!" says Lula. "But are they just stories or are there real knights, doing really brave things, in other parts of the world too?"

"Of course there are!" says Sir Eustace. "Look!"

Flowering Knights or Hwarang

Noble warriors from ancient Korea, trained in the arts as well as fighting.

Bound by honour, duty and brotherhood.

Usama ibn Munqidh

A great faris (Muslim knight) and poet.

Grew up in the castle of Shayzar in Syria.

Wrote the story of his life, serving many lords in many battles.

Mubarizun

The most fearsome warriors in the early Islamic world.

Before any battle, they would fight the champions of the enemy army in single combat.

The Eso Ikoyi

Military elite of the Yoruba empire of Oyo in West Africa.

Famous for their code of honour, called Emi Omo Eso.

Kheshig

The most skilful soldiers in the Mongol empire (one of the largest empires in history, stretching from the Sea of Japan to Eastern Europe).

Rewarded with money and honours.

Personal bodyguards of Genghis Khan, founder of the empire.

Wonhwa ("Original Flowers")

Three hundred girls from the ancient kingdom of Silla, in Korea.

Chosen for their beauty and battle skills.

Samurai

A powerful class of warriors from Japan.

Served a lord and lived in his castle.

Fearsome in battle and bound by a code of honour, called Bushido.

Samurai armour is made of iron plates so it can move easily.

Ronin (Wandering Samurai)

When the samurais' lord died and had no heir to take his place, the samurai became 'ronin' (knights without a lord) and were left to travel all over Japan, fighting for many different masters and armies.

MAKING HISTORY

THE GREAT KNIGHTS OF THE PAST

"So knights exist all over the world!" says Lula.

"History is full of brave people," says Sir Eustace.

"Who are the most famous knights of all?" asks Jake.

"There's a long list," replies Sir Eustace, "but here are a few whose names will be remembered forever."

RODRIGO DÍAZ DE VIVAR, 'EL CID'

Spanish knight who fought for both Christian and Muslim armies. Ruled over a city in which people from different cultures could live together in peace.

WILLIAM MARSHAL, ENGLAND'S BEST KNIGHT

A successful tournament knight who went on to fight for five different English kings.

BERTRAND DU GUESCLIN, 'THE EAGLE OF BRITTANY'

French national hero. Fought bravely against the English in the Hundred Years' War.

JOAN OF ARC

A farmer's daughter who became patron saint of France. She wasn't a knight, but her courage and faith inspired armies. Other women were just as brave as knights such as...

Ruler of Tuscany, in Northern Italy. Fought for the Pope and to defend her lands against the Emperor Henry IV. Known as 'the Great Countess' for her strength and bravery.

First Queen of a united Spain. Appeared in full armour to encourage her troops in battle. Encouraged explorers to go on voyages of discovery.

Chivalry

"Knights are not just warriors," Sir Eustace explains. "We are all bound by a code of honour, called chivalry. To be a knight is to be brave and fair, loyal and generous, to protect the weak and fight for what's good. Sometimes, knights join together in orders of chivalry such as these."

Order of the Garter

Founded by Edward III of England.

To help Edward become king of France.

Celebrated with feasting and jousting.

Order of the Golden Fleece

Founded by Philip, Duke of Burgundy.

To honour the noble order of knighthood.

Knights would be asked about going to war, and disputes between knights would be settled by the order, not law courts.

Order of the Star

Founded by King John II of France.

To reward loyalty to the King and protect France from the English.

Knights swore never to retreat from a battle.

LET THE GAMES BEGIN!

CELEBRATING WITH A TOURNAMENT

The kids hear the sound of trumpets from outside.

"The Baron is celebrating his return home with a tournament," says Sir Eustace. "I have to go and get ready."

"We don't want to miss this!" says Jake.

They follow the crowds who are gathering to watch.

Jousting started as battle practice – many battles were won by a lot of knights charging at once.

The little wooden fence in the middle is called the 'tilt'.

Knights charge on the right-hand side of the tilt.

A knight is allowed three lances. If they break all three and there's still no winner, the fight continues on foot with blunted swords.

In England, King Edward I banned the spectators from having weapons in case they wanted to join in too!

GOOD NEWS!

You're a knight in a joust – everyone's turned out to see how brave you are.

BAD NEWS!

You're facing a fearsome rival.

GOOD NEWS!

The pointy end of your rival's lance is capped.

BAD NEWS!

Being hit with a lance still delivers an almighty THWACK!

The people who are in charge – such as the Baron and his wife – watch the joust from a covered stand.

Squires are on hand to supply their knight with new weapons and armour.

Lady's Favour

Some knights fight to prove their love. They wear a 'favour' (a ribbon, a handkerchief or a glove) to show which lady they are fighting for. If they win, they might get a kiss.

GOOD NEWS!

If you win, you might get money or jewels.

BAD NEWS!

The prize in one tournament wasn't money or jewels – it was a peacock!

A GOODBYE FEAST

It's getting late and Jake and Lula's tummies are rumbling again. The Baron is holding a great feast in the hall and Lula and Jake are invited to join as guests.

"I can't wait for the big feast!" says Jake. "Will there be pizza?"

"What's pizza?" asks Hubert.

"Huh?! No pizza? What are we going to eat?" asks Jake.

"The Baron's favourite food is pork, eggs, currants and dates boiled together in a bladder, which is then sliced and eaten in sauce."

"Bleurgh!" says Jake.

"Will there be other food to eat besides... erm... bladder?" asks Lula.

"There will be lots of boiled, baked and roasted meat," says Hubert. "As well as fish, baked and stewed fruit, and cheese."

Meat is cooked with dried fruit, and plenty of spices such as cinnamon, cumin, liquorice, ginger, coriander, nutmeg and cloves.

Forks are used in the kitchen but most people won't use forks to eat with for another 100 years.

Food arrives in sharing bowls. People serve themselves. It's bad manners to take all the best bits for yourself.

People are seated in order of their importance. The Baron and his wife have the best spot – sitting right in the middle of the most important table. They will be served first and have the best view of the entertainment.

Minstrels play music from a special gallery.

Henry II of England had a jester called Ronald the Farter. Every Christmas he had to perform 'one jump and whistle and one fart'.

TABLE MANNERS

Wash your hands before and after dinner.

Take food OFF your knife to eat it.

Don't fill your mouth with food.

Don't wipe your mouth on your sleeve – use a napkin.

No spitting or belching at the table!

BEDTIME!

Jake and Lula have had so many adventures in the Middle Ages, but now it's time for their sleepover.

"These beds have curtains!" says Jake. "We can play hide-and-seek!"

"The curtains are designed to keep you warm in a draughty castle," explains Hubert.

"And besides," says Eloise. "You've just given away your hiding place!"

"What shall we do then?" asks Lula. "I'm far too excited to sleep."

"Would you like to take a souvenir home?" asks Eloise.

"I'd like that balloon thing the jester has please," says Jake.

"His bladder, you mean?" says Hubert.

"As long as you promise not to bop me on the head with it," says Lula.

"Oh all right!" says Jake.

"I'd like a knight's shield please," says Lula. "If I hold it up in front of my face, I won't have to watch Jake's 'jump, whistle and fart' jester dance."

THE SLEEPOVER'S OVER!

THANKS FOR HAVING US

The next morning, it's time for our travellers to go home.

"That was a very comfy bed," says Lula, "until the bedbugs got me."

"Hubert and Eloise, you must come and visit us sometime," says Jake.

"Oh yes," says Lula. "I'd love to show you phones, and the games you can play on them, and trains. They're like carriages without horses that whizz along rails at 100 miles an hour."

"No one can travel that fast!" says Hubert.

"Just you wait," says Lula.

"But how will we visit you?" asks Eloise.

"Time travel," say Lula and Jake. "It's easy...